So you want to be a Cartoonist?

by PETER ·MADDOCKS·

FIRST PUBLISHED IN GREAT BRITAIN IN 1998 BY:
MICHAEL O'MARA BOOKS LIMITED
9 LION YARD
TREMADOC ROAD
LONDON SW4 7NQ

SO YOU WANT TO BE A CARTOONIST?
©1998 BY PETER MADDOCKS

A CIP CATALOGUE RECORD FOR THIS BOOK
IS AVAILABLE FROM THE BRITISH LIBRARY.

ISBN 1-85479-391-8

1 3 5 7 9 10 8 6 4 2
PRINTED AND BOUND BY WSOY, FINLAND.

LET'S START IN THE BEGINNING—
BUT THIS TIME, LET US USE PEN
AND PAPER

CLEVER CARTOONISTS USE THE OLD FASHIONED INK DIP PEN

YOU CAN ALWAYS RECOGNISE THEM BY THEIR INKY FINGERS...

BLACK DRAWING INK FROM THE POT OR BOTTLE IS USUALLY PERMANENT BLACK

*THAT MEANS IT <u>NEVER</u> FADES!

AND OF COURSE, THE SCRATCH PEN NIB WILL GIVE YOU A SPLENDID VARIATION OF LINE THAT ART LOVERS ADORE ——→

HOWEVER, TODAYS PENS ARE SO EASY TO USE, SO CLEAN AND SO FAST TO DRY THAT YOU CAN ALMOST FINISH A DRAWING BEFORE CLEVER CLOGS CAN GET THE CAP OFF THE INK BOTTLE ——

YOU CAN BUY THIS KIND OF PEN ALMOST ANYWHERE THESE DAYS

I LIKE A PILOT DRAWING PEN NUMBERS ONE TO EIGHT...

NUMBERS ONE TO EIGHT WILL GIVE YOU A WIDE
VARIATION OF LINE — ONE TO THREE FOR
VERY FINE LINE DRAWING — FOUR OR FIVE FOR
OUTLINE AND NUMBERS SIX, SEVEN OR EIGHT
FOR FILLING IN. "

THE INK IS PERMANENT WITH AN EXCELLENT
BLACK LINE — ALL THE WORK IN THIS
BOOK, INCLUDING THE LETTERING IS
DONE WITH PILOT DRAWING PENS...

I ALWAYS DRAW ON A
GOOD QUALITY COPYING
PAPER — ULTRA WHITE
A4 OR A3 100 GSM...

IT DOESN'T BLEED — AND YOU'VE ALWAYS
GOT PLENTY OF IT IF YOU BUY 500 SHEET
PACKS — AND NO TEARS IF YOU MAKE
A BOO BOO! ⁆⁅ G*☆!!

WHAT ME?
NEVER!

I ALWAYS DRAW DIRECT WITH A PEN——
BUT IF YOU MUST USE A PENCIL TO SKETCH
OR ROUGH OUT YOUR DRAWING (AND WHY NOT?)

HB ✓   ~~2B~~

THEN MAKE SURE YOU USE AN HB LEAD
OTHERWISE YOU'LL MUCK EVERYTHING
UP BY TRYING TO CLEAN OFF HEAVY
PENCIL MARKS WITH YOUR ERASER!

ANY MISTAKES —— CLEAN UP WITH A
MICRO CORRECT PEN
IT LOOKS LIKE A
FAT PEN WITH
A FINE POINT

WHITE

SHAKE
SHAKE

MAJOR MISTAKES (EITHER SCRAP AND
START AGAIN) OR——CUT AND STICK FRESH
PATCHES OF PAPER AND RE-DRAW.
(THE BENEFIT OF USING COPY PAPER AND
 NOT EXPENSIVE DRAWING CARD)

STICK

IF YOU HAVE THE USE OF
A COPYING MACHINE——
(AND HOW DID I EVER MANAGE
 WITHOUT ONE IN THE GOOD OLD
 DIP-PEN AND BLOT DAYS?)

YOUR CORRECTING WILL NOT BE A PROBLEM,
JUST WHITE OUT——COPY——AND CONTINUE
WITH THE DRAWING...

OKAY — NOW YOU KNOW WHAT MATERIALS TO USE — SO CLEAR THE TABLE, DESK OR DRAWING BOARD — WE ARE NOW GOING TO DRAW CARTOONS

WHAT SIZE DO I DRAW?

DO I FILL THE WHOLE PAGE?

DO I DRAW A BORDER?

HOW BIG SHOULD MY CARTOON BE?

UPRIGHT OR OBLONG?

IF WE START DRAWING ON A4 COPY PAPER
— GET YOURSELF A PIECE OF A4 CARD.
(NOT TOO STIFF) EASY TO CUT —

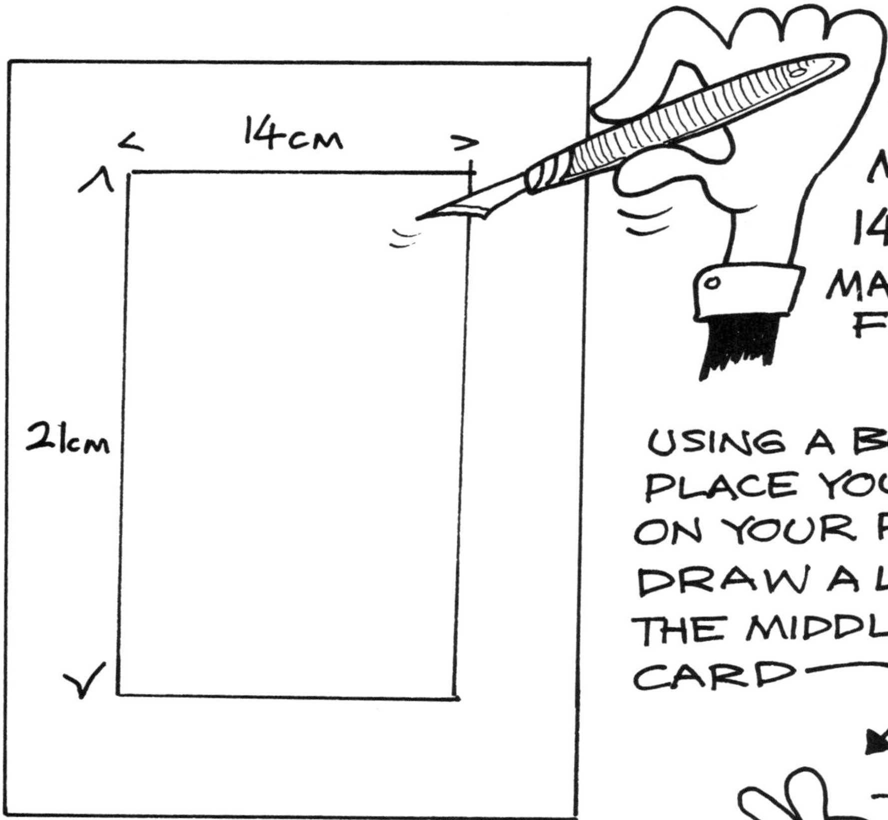

CUT OUT
THE MIDDLE
MEASURING
14cm X 21cm
MAKING A
FRAME !

14cm

21cm

USING A BLUE PENCIL
PLACE YOUR FRAME
ON YOUR PAPER AND
DRAW A LINE AROUND
THE MIDDLE OF THE
CARD —

EASY!

FRAME CARD

THE BLUE PENCIL FRAME ON YOUR PAPER
GIVES YOU A SHAPE TO DRAW WITHIN—
EITHER PORTRAIT OR LANDSCAPE
(UPRIGHT OR OBLONG)

THE BLUE PENCIL LINE DOESN'T REPRODUCE
IF PHOTOGRAPHED FOR PUBLICATION.
THE FRAME WILL HELP YOU CONTROL THE
SIZE AND SHAPE OF YOUR DRAWING

* VERY IMPORTANT IF YOU HOPE TO SELL
YOUR WORK BECAUSE ART EDITORS ARE
OBSESSED BY SIZE & SHAPE OF A
CARTOON FAR MORE THAN ITS CONTENT!

OKAY! —NOW WHERE DO I START?

WELL — I START WITH THE NOSE —

THEN I ADD THE EYES

FOLLOWED BY THE HEAD

CHANGE THE HAIR STYLE

VARY IT A LITTLE...

MALE

OR FEMALE

IT'S A VERY SIMPLE DRAWING STYLE

TRY IT!

WORRY ABOUT DEVELOPING YOUR OWN STYLE LATER —— IT'S GREAT FUN...

TRY LOTS OF FACES — ADD GLASSES, HATS,
MOUSTACHES, BEARDS — CHANGE HAIR STYLES
MALE, FEMALE, YOUNG OR OLD THE
DRAWING TECHNIQUE IS THE SAME...

NECK LINES
ADD AGE

HAPPY
OR
SAD

YOUNG
OR
OLD

SPORTY
OR
NOT

HAT OR
HELMETS

SAINT OR
SINNER

KEEP AT IT — FACES TELL A STORY
TRY LOTS OF EXPRESSIONS — LOOK IN THE
MIRROR AND PULL FACES — YOU'LL BE
SURPRISED HOW FRIGHTENING YOU CAN
LOOK —

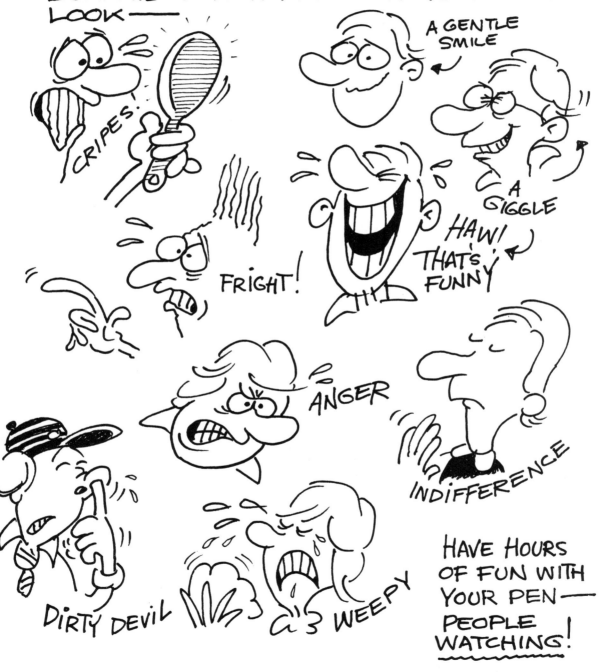

CRIPES!

A GENTLE SMILE

A GIGGLE

FRIGHT!

HAW! THAT'S FUNNY

ANGER

INDIFFERENCE

DIRTY DEVIL

3 WEEPY

HAVE HOURS OF FUN WITH YOUR PEN — PEOPLE WATCHING!

BODY LANGUAGE — WATCH PEOPLE AT
WORK AND AT PLAY — SEE HOW THEY
REACT TO ANY SITUATION... IT'S
GREAT FUN, PEOPLE WATCHING —

KEEP YOUR PEN OR PENCIL BUSY SKETCHING
DOWN WHAT YOU SEE — IT'S GOOD REFERENCE

SIMPLE OUTLINE DRAWINGS WILL GIVE YOU
ALL THE EXPRESSION YOU NEED TO CONVEY
A SITUATION —

I ALWAYS DRAW THE FEMALE MUCH TALLER THAN THE MALE — TAKE A LOOK AT THE SIZE OF THOSE GIRLS COMING OUT OF SCHOOL THESE DAYS — IT'S ONLY WHEN THEY GET TO BE LITTLE OLD LADIES THAT THEY SHRINK — OR ARE THEY TWO SEPARATE SPECIES ?

WATCH PEOPLE AT WORK—— UNIFORMS ARE ALWAYS USEFUL, THE POSTMAN, THE MILKMAN, THE VICAR OR THE PARKING METER LADY—— YOU'LL NEED ALL THESE CHARACTERS IN YOUR CARTOONS...

THEY DON'T HAVE TO BE ACCURATE, JUST ENOUGH TO SHOW WHO IT IS——

ABOVE ALL — PUT ANIMATION INTO YOUR
CHARACTERS — MAKE THEM LOOK AS IF
THEY ARE MOVING, NOTHING PUTS YOU
OFF A CARTOON MORE THAN WOODEN
LOOKING DRAWINGS...

SPEED LINES AND
SWEAT MARKS ALL
HELP TO SHOW
MOVEMENT AND
MAKE YOUR DRAWING
MORE INTERESTING
TO LOOK AT...

SPORT IS A GREAT CANVAS FOR ACTION,
ALMOST ANY SPORTING ACTIVITY WILL
CREATE ROOM FOR THE MOST ANIMATED
FIGURE — PICK A SPORT—AND DRAW.

HANDS ARE VERY IMPORTANT TO EXPRESS
ACTION AND MOVEMENT—DON'T NEGLECT
OR TRY TO HIDE THEM — KEEP THEM
SIMPLE BUT USE THEM FOR EFFECT...

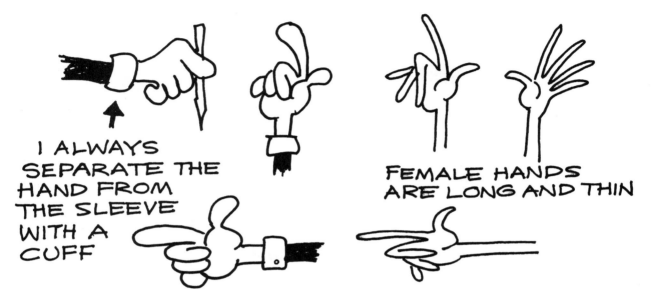

I ALWAYS
SEPARATE THE
HAND FROM
THE SLEEVE
WITH A
CUFF

FEMALE HANDS
ARE LONG AND THIN

WORK AT IT UNTIL YOU GET THE HANDS
LOOKING RIGHT——NOTHING LOOKS WORSE
THAN BADLY DRAWN HANDS—REMEMBER

① BACK OF HANDS
(THUMBS FACE INWARDS)

② PALM OF HANDS
(THUMBS FACE OUTWARDS)

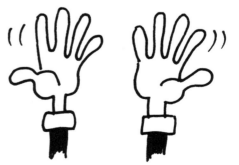

NOW, PRACTICE DRAWING HANDS—

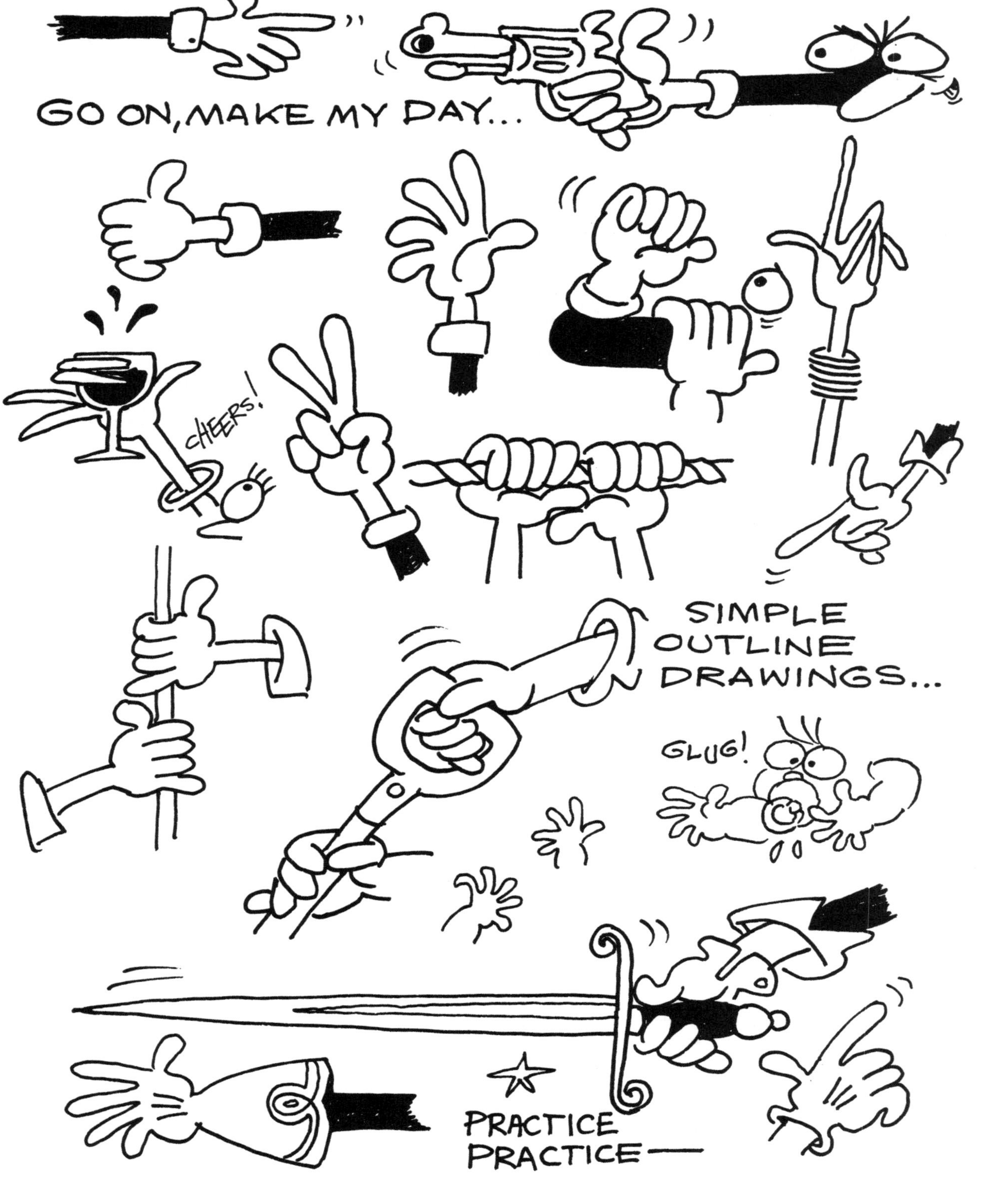

☆ CHECK YOUR ACTION IN A MIRROR
THEN SIT DOWN AND DRAW IT!

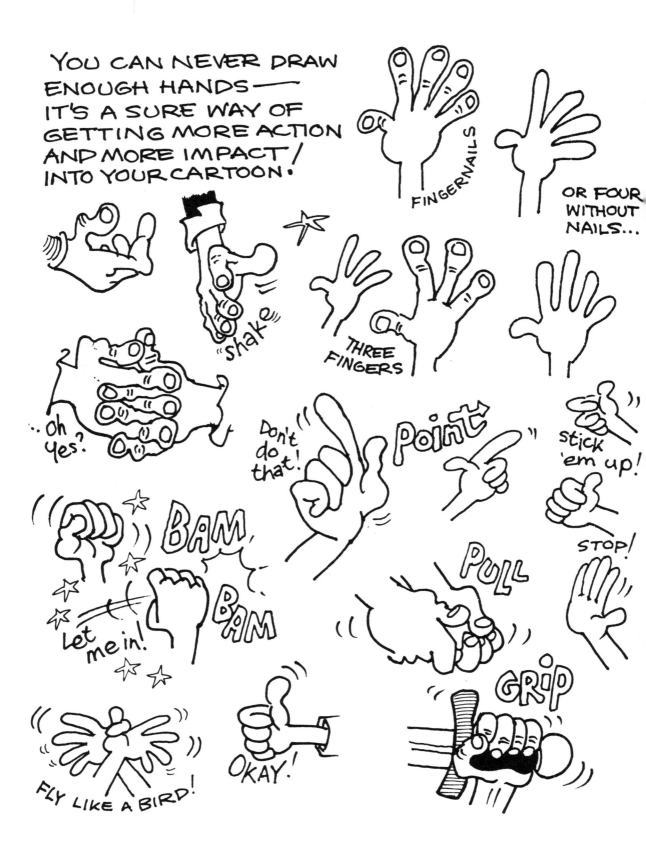

FEET ALSO NEED ATTENTION—YOU CAN HAVE FUN FOLLOWING THE CRAZY FASHION FADS AS THEY COME AND GO...

SOME SHOES

FORE!

— ARE A WORK OF ART!

WHAT STYLE SHALL I DRAW IN?

BIG NOSES

BIG EYES

SQUARE HEAD

ROUND HEAD

POINTED

OR OBLONG?

DON'T WORRY ABOUT IT — JUST KEEP DRAWING, IF YOU DO TEND TO HAVE A STYLE OF YOUR OWN — IT WILL COME THROUGH AS YOU PROGRESS — JUST LIKE HANDWRITING...

SO DON'T WORRY ABOUT IT——:

IF IT'S THERE——IT WILL SHOW THROUGH!

HOWEVER—WHEN YOU DO FIND A STYLE—

STICK WITH IT—
BUT DON'T CUT YOUR EAR OFF!

DRAWING CHILDREN —

YOU NEED TO EXAGGERATE EXPRESSIONS
EVEN MORE THAN USUAL WHEN DRAWING
THE LITTLE PEOPLE — GO WAY OVER THE TOP!

DON'T HOLD BACK — GO FOR IT!

TRY DRAWING CHILDREN OF ALL AGES AND GROUPS...

KEEP THEM SIMPLE IN OUTLINE —

NICE HEAVY TYPE FOOTWEAR ALWAYS LOOKS RIGHT ON BOYS. (SNEAKERS)

FOR DARKER SKIN USE EITHER A TINT OR LINES (AS ABOVE)

GIVE THE BOYS LARGER HEADS
AND BAGGY PANTS WITH CLUMSY FEET

GIRLS ARE MORE
LEGGY THAN BOYS —
AND OF COURSE A
LOT CUTER —
THEY SMILE A LOT

AND LITTLE
BOYS
PONG!
A LOT!

MORE KIDS FACES...

YOU CAN NEVER DRAW ENOUGH FACES...

TEENAGERS

TEENAGERS ARE CHILDREN WITH FULL SIZE FIGURES, THEY HAVE A DRESS CODE ALL OF THEIR OWN ——

TRY TO IMAGINE THEM AS TINY TOTS AND THEN DRAW THEM AGAIN AS THE GROWN-UP VERSION...

AGAIN—IT'S EXPRESSIONS THAT ARE IMPORTANT— LET THE DRAWING TELL THE STORY—AND THE CAPTION TELL THE GAG.

YOUNG FACES FOR YOUR FILE...

I LIKE TO PUT A LOT OF EXPRESSION INTO THE EYES — IT'S A SIMPLE TECHNIQUE BUT VERY EFFECTIVE — EVEN WHEN WEARING GLASSES...

STEREOTYPES

THERE IS A BAND OF PEOPLE WHO WILL ALWAYS POP UP IN YOUR CARTOONS FROM TIME TO TIME— SO IT'S A GOOD IDEA TO GET A ROUGH IDEA ON DRESS— UNIFORMS ETC...

GOTCHA!

PARKI

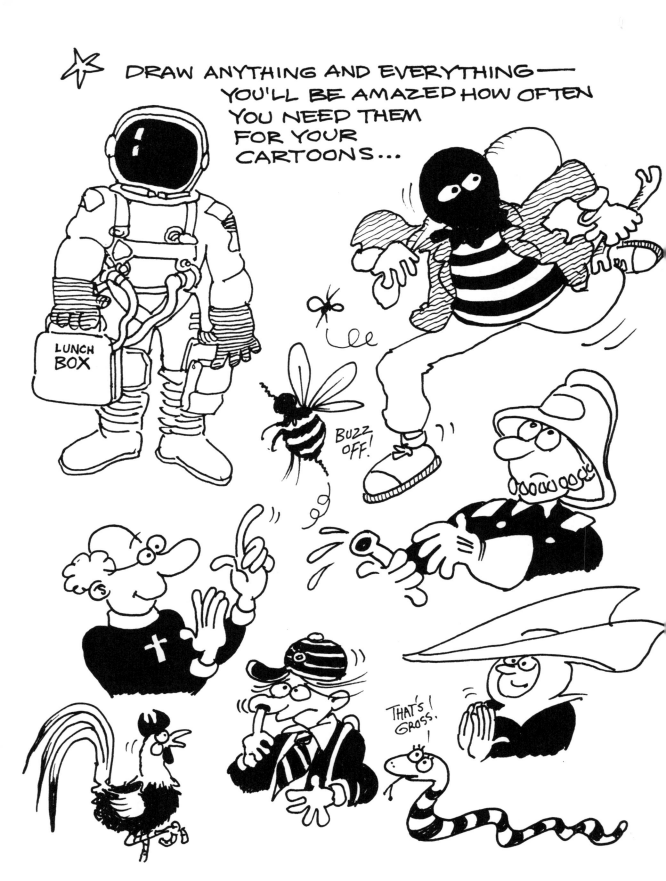

AN IDEA FOR A CARTOON WILL COME TO
YOU WHEN YOU LEAST EXPECT IT—BEWARE!
DON'T THINK YOU CAN CARRY IT AROUND IN
YOUR HEAD UNTIL YOU GET TO YOUR
DRAWING BOARD, BECAUSE YOU'LL LOSE IT.
SOMETHING ELSE WILL BLOCK IT OUT FOR
EVER—WRITE IT DOWN, EVEN IF YOUR
POCKETS ARE STUFFED WITH BITS OF
PAPER, IT DOESN'T MATTER—AND EVEN
WHEN YOU COME TO DRAW IT YOU MAY
GET A DIFFERENT SLANT ON IT TO WHAT
YOU ORIGINALLY THOUGHT—BUT THE
IDEA YOU HAD IS THERE ON PAPER...

I'VE EVEN GOT OUT OF
BED IN THE EARLY HOURS
WITH A GAG IDEA IN MY
HEAD—I MAKE FOR THE
LOO AND JOT IT DOWN
ON TOILET PAPER IN
THE DARK— IT'S
THERE IN THE MORNING!

DON'T BE TOO HASTY TO DISMISS AN IDEA,
DRAW IT UP—AND TAKE A LOOK AT IT
A COUPLE OF DAYS LATER— IF IT
DOESN'T WORK, YOU'LL PROBABLY SEE
WHY—AND A SMALL CORRECTION
WILL MAKE IT A WINNER!

—NO MORE BOTTLE BANKS, SON!

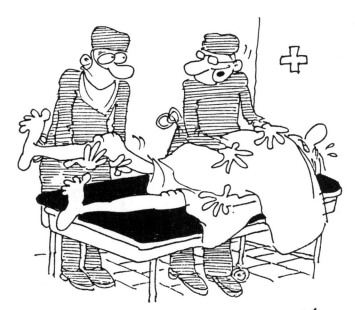

IF HE WORKS IN THE TREASURY
—HE'LL MAKE A VERY SLOW RECOVERY!

WHEN WRITING GAG CAPTIONS, TRY TO
KEEP THEM AS SHORT AS POSSIBLE—
AND TO THE POINT.
LONG CAPTIONS ONLY LOOK LABOURED,
I SAY, A READER WILL SPEND NO MORE
THAN THIRTY SECONDS LOOKING AT A
CARTOON — SO THE QUICKER IT MAKES
ITS MARK, THE BETTER.

HERE ARE A SELECTION OF GAG CAPTIONS
TO SET YOUR IMAGINATION GOING—
STUDY THE CAPTION AND COME UP WITH
A VISUAL TO ILLUSTRATE IT — YOU'LL BE
AMAZED AT HOW MANY VARIATIONS
YOU CAN GET FROM ONE CAPTION.

A QUESTION ALWAYS ASKED IS WHAT
COMES FIRST— THE CAPTION OR THE
VISUAL — WELL, BEING A NEWSPAPER
CARTOONIST, I'D SAY THE CAPTION—
HOWEVER, I'M A GREAT FAN OF THE
CAPTION-LESS CARTOON — BUT WE'LL
COME TO THAT LATER...

DON'T TRY AND BE TOO CLEVER—
READ A CAPTION, THINK OF A VISUAL
AND DRAW IT UP AS A CARTOON.

THINK PICTURES...

CARTOON CAPTIONS

"STEP OUTSIDE AND SAY THAT!"

"TURN YOUR FACE TO THE WALL!"

"—MIRROR, MIRROR, ON THE WALL"

"ASK YOUR FRIEND TO USE THE OTHER BAR!"

"HOLD EVERYTHING—IT HAS SIDE EFFECTS!"

"THE LAST TIME I SAW YOU—YOU WERE SO HIGH!"

"LAST ONE IN—FIRST ONE OUT!"

"HE HAS SUCH DEEP TASTE BUDS!"

"LOOK AT ME WHEN I'M TALKING TO YOU"

"I THINK I'M GOING THATAWAY!"

"I AM THE GHOST OF CHRISTMAS YET TO COME!"

"MY GOODNESS—ISN'T HE LIKE HIS DAD?"

THINK PICTURES

—YOU'VE NEVER HEARD OF A
PIGGY-BACK?

THINK PICTURES!

—WHICH OLD BOOT DO YOU MEAN, SIR?

WOULD YOU MIND—ONLY I'VE LOST MY DIPSTICK!

"HIM SPEAK WITH FORKED FINGERS!"

"YOU CALL YOURSELF A DRIVER?"

"HAVE YOU A BANKERS CARD, SIR?"

"CAN I HAVE A WORD WITH THE LITTLE WOMAN?"

"HE MAKES ALL HIS OWN BEER!"

"ARE YOU A QUALIFIED OPTICIAN?"

THE Visual CARTOON... (NO CAPTION)

VISUAL GAGS — THE CARTOON WITHOUT A CAPTION IS REALLY THE TRUE CARTOON. IF YOU ARE SERIOUS ABOUT BEING A CARTOONIST — DRAW AS MANY VISUAL CARTOONS AS YOU CAN — THEY NEED NO WORDS, NO TRANSLATION, NO LANGUAGE THEY WILL SELL AROUND THE WORLD — HUMOUR IS INTERNATIONAL."

THEY ARE NOT EASY TO THINK UP — THEY NEED TO HAVE IMMEDIATE IMPACT. THINK BACK TO THOSE WONDERFUL SILENT COMEDIES OF THE EARLY FILMS — THEY HAVE SURVIVED THE TEST OF TIME.

I ALWAYS SAY, PUT A GOOD VISUAL GAG IN A DRAWER AND OPEN IT TWENTY YEARS LATER AND THERE IS STILL A SMILE IN THAT DRAWER!

WHEN DRAWING A VISUAL CARTOON YOU MUST MAKE SURE THAT THE POINT OF THE GAG IS VERY CLEAR — DON'T OVERDRAW SO THAT YOU COMPLICATE THE CARTOON. KEEP AN OPEN LINE WHERE POSSIBLE USING SOLID BLACK TO POINT OUT THE GAG — THE LESS COMPLICATED THE CARTOON — THE BETTER...

SOMETIMES YOU MAY HAVE TO SPELL OUT A VISUAL GAG WITH A WRITTEN SIGN WITHIN THE DRAWING. —THAT'S OKAY— BUT BANG GOES YOUR FOREIGN SALES...

CHICKEN LEGS

OUT OF WORK! OUT OF MONEY! OUT OF TUNE!

THANK YOU

UNEMPLOYED GUY

TO MAKE YOUR CARTOONS LOOK MORE INTERESTING
TRY TO VARY THE ANGLE OF YOUR ARTWORK—
TAKE A SLANT FROM ABOVE OR BELOW FOR A
CHANGE—SWITCH THE EYE LEVEL...
IT CAN GIVE A DRAWING A LOT MORE IMPACT!

TRY OUT A FEW ROUGHS DRAWING DIFFERENT ANGLES — IF YOU WANT GOOD EXAMPLES OF THIS KIND OF ARTWORK TAKE A LOOK AT THE GRAPHIC NOVELS IN YOUR LOCAL BOOKSHOP OR LIBRARY.

IT'S NOT EASY—BUT IF YOU GET IT RIGHT IT'S VERY SATISFYING—GET IT WRONG, AND IT LOOKS LIKE NOTHING ON EARTH! GREAT TECHNIQUE FOR ILLUSTRATING A GRIPPING YARN IN A BOOK OR COMIC.

BACKGROUNDS—
SETTING THE SCENE IS A WAY OF TELLING
YOUR READERS WHERE YOUR CHARACTERS
ARE WITHIN THE FRAME OF YOUR CARTOON.

WATERFALL

WHIRLPOOL

SHARK

PIRATES

YOU CAN USE A FEW PROPS LIKE A TELEPHONE OR A T/V SET OR SHOW A DOOR WITH A SIGN ON IT—BUT WHATEVER YOU DRAW IT MUST INFORM YOUR READER AS TO WHERE YOUR CHARACTERS ARE SITUATED WITHIN YOUR CARTOON—

FREEZE UP

A RIVER

A STAIRCASE

A BEACH

A PARK

A WINDOW

A ROUGH SEA

IF YOU ARE USING WRITTEN SIGNS—DON'T
DO MIRROR WRITING ON THE WINDOWS...
BACKWARDS WRITING WILL NOT ONLY LOOK
WRONG, IT WILL DISTRACT YOUR READER
FROM WHERE AND WHAT YOUR CARTOON IS
ABOUT——IF IT'S A BANK—SAY BANK!

LIMITED SPACE DICTATES HOW MUCH DETAIL YOU CAN PUT INTO YOUR BACKGROUND—AND IT MUST NOT GET IN THE WAY OF YOUR CHARACTERS——SO EVERY DETAIL MUST SPELL OUT WHAT IS HAPPENING——SNOW, RAIN, FLOOD OR JUST A SUNNY DAY—IT HAS TO INFORM YOUR READER OF THE SITUATION...

SNOW

STORM

HEAT

FLOODS

IF YOU HAVE TROUBLE DRAWING
ANIMAL FACES — TRY THIS SIMPLE
FACE — TWO EYES, A NOSE AND A MOUTH

IT FITS
ALMOST ANY
FACE FOR
ANY ANIMAL!

HEY!

YOU CAN MOVE
THE NOSE ABOUT.

KEEP DRAWING FACES AND LET YOUR
IMAGINATION RUN RIOT—STRETCH
IT TO THE LIMIT—AND BEYOND...

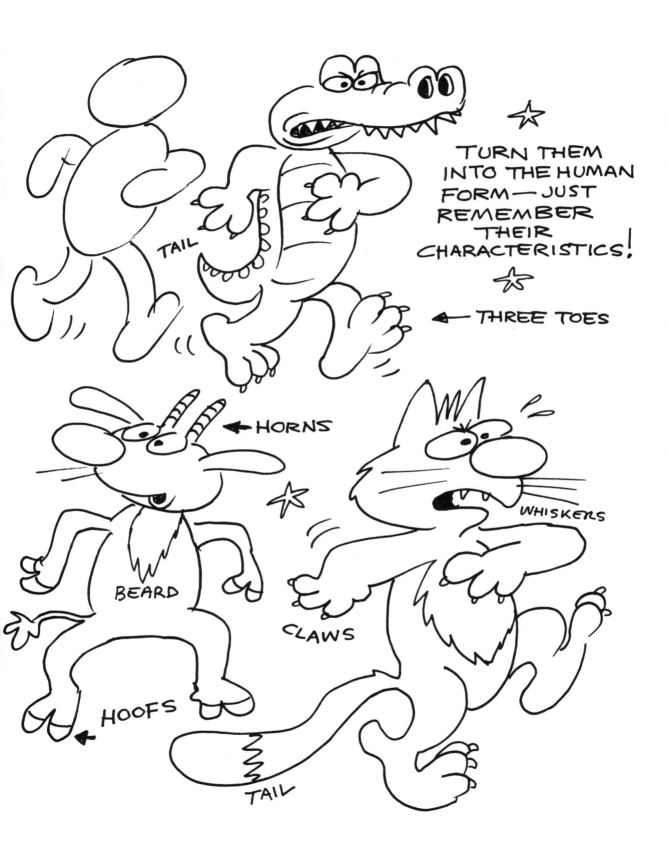

TAKE THE HUMAN FIGURE AND TRANSFORM IT

PHEW!

ANTHROPOMORPHISM!

THIS MEANS HUMANISING THINGS OTHER THAN PEOPLE — CARTOON ANIMALS CAN BE DRAWN WITH THE SAME HUMAN ATTRIBUTES —

YOU HAVE TO KNOW HOW TO DRAW HUMANS TO DO THIS OF COURS

YOU CAN HAVE LOTS OF FUN WITH ANIMALS BY TURNING THEM INTO JOKE CHARACTERS— IDEAL FOR KIDDIES BOOKS OR COMICS...

Turtle-Dove

Cat-Fish

TRY A FEW OF THESE...

IT WILL STRETCH YOUR IMAGINATION!

Fox-Glove

Jelly-Fish

Door-Mouse

HOWEVER—IF YOU WANT YOUR CARTOON ANIMALS TO LOOK LIKE ANIMALS— THEN I SUGGEST YOU VISIT A ZOO WITH YOUR SKETCH BOOK—OR EVEN POP OUT TO YOUR NEAREST COUNTRY FARM...

MOOOO

★ ALWAYS USEFUL

★ START A REFERENCE BOOK OF SKETCHES!

BUT ABOVE ALL, GET CRACKING ON
ANIMAL CARTOON DRAWINGS ——
YOU WILL BE SURPRISED HOW OFTEN
YOU NEED TO USE THEM IN YOUR GAGS!

THE BEST TECHNIQUE YOU CAN EVER USE
FOR CARTOONS TO BE REPRODUCED IN
NEWSPAPERS OR MAGAZINES—— IS
A GOOD STRONG OUTLINE WITH SOLID
BLACK AS A FILLER—
HOWEVER, THERE ARE OTHER TECHNIQUES
YOU CAN USE SHOULD YOUR STYLE OF
DRAWING REQUIRE IT——

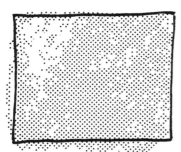

INSTANTEX——
BUY IT IN SHEETS
AND JUST RUB IT ON.

BLUE PENCIL
TO INDICATE
WHERE YOU WANT
A TINT.

FINGER DIPPED
IN BLACK—
MESSY BUT
VERY ARTY!

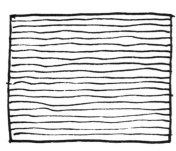

STRAIGHT LINES
ALWAYS WORK
WELL...

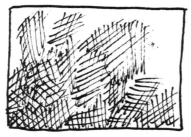

CROSS HATCHING
LOOKS GOOD IF
NOT OVERDONE.

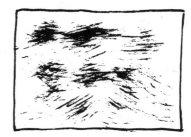

STIPPLE OR
DRY BRUSH...

LINE & SOLID BLACK

LINE & SOLID BLACK

A GOOD LINE PLUS
SOLID BLACK WILL
JUMP OFF THE
PAGE EVERY TIME!

THE TOPICAL CARTOON.

UNLESS A NEWSPAPER EDITOR INVITES
YOU TO PRODUCE A DAILY/WEEKLY
TOPICAL CARTOON FOR HIS PAPER
OR MAGAZINE — OFFERING YOU A REALLY
WORTHWHILE FEE (BOTH UNLIKELY)—
DON'T BOTHER—— THE DAILY SLOG
OF COMING UP WITH A SELECTION OF
ROUGHS (ABOUT SIX) SO THAT AN
EDITOR (WHO IS A WORDSMITH ANYWAY)
CAN CHOOSE ONE — FOR YOU TO GO
AWAY AND DRAW UP—AND EVEN
THEN, HOPE THEY CAN FIND SPACE FOR
IT—OR HAS THE NEWS ITEM YOU
BASED YOUR CARTOON ON CHANGED,
OR BEEN DROPPED FROM THE PAPER?

BE WARNED! IF YOU WANT ULCERS—OR WORSE...

THIS IS THE JOB FOR YOU (POOR SOUL!)

FORGET IT! AND STAY HAPPY!

HOWEVER—IF YOU DO GET OFFERED THE JOB AS A TOPICAL CARTOONIST!

BEWARE OF TALKING HEADS—IF EVERY DAY YOUR VISUAL IS TWO HEADS IN CONVERSATION— NO MATTER HOW WITTY THE CAPTION, IT CAN LOOK VERY BORING!

TRY TO MAKE YOUR CARTOON INTERESTING TO LOOK AT EACH DAY.

AND IF YOU TAKE MY ADVICE—STICK TO DRAWING GAGS THAT MAKE PEOPLE LAUGH (OR JUST AMUSE YOURSELF) HEH HEH!

HERE READS A VERY BRILLIANT, PUNCHY TOPICAL CAPTION ON A SUBJECT EVERY READER IS AWARE OF (YOU HOPE!)

THE DAILY TOPICAL GAG IS A SURE WAY OF DRAINING OUT ANY TALENT OR STYLE OR ENTHUSIASM YOU EVER HAD IN THE FIRST PLACE!

THE SPORTS CARTOON HAS LOST FAVOUR
IN OUR NEWSPAPERS THESE DAYS —
IT'S A PITY, BECAUSE THIS IS AN AREA
FOR LOADS OF CARTOON HUMOUR, AND
I'M CONVINCED IT WILL RETURN AS SOON
AS EDITORS REALISE THAT MONEY
DOMINATED SPORT IS LOSING ITS
SENSE OF HUMOUR —

"RELAX BOSS —
IT'S ONLY BRAIN DAMAGE"

"WITH THOSE FEET,
HE'LL NEVER CATCH
HIM —"

"HORSES — SOMETIMES — JOCKEYS, NEVER!"

THE SPORTING CARICATURE

YOU EITHER HAVE THE GIFT FOR CAPTURING A LIKENESS — OR YOU HAVEN'T. I AM NOT A NATURAL CARICATURIST, SO I HAVE TO WORK HARD AT IT — BUT WHEN I DO EVENTUALLY GET IT RIGHT IT IS VERY REWARDING.

FOOTBALL CARICATURES ARE ALWAYS IN DEMAND, BUT BEWARE — BECAUSE THEY DO TEND TO CHANGE STRIPS OR CLUBS AT THE DROP OF A COIN...

THE HEAD ALWAYS LOOKS BETTER WHEN IT IS MUCH LARGER IN PROPORTION THAN THE BODY — IT ALSO GIVES THE READER MORE OPPORTUNITY TO RECOGNISE WHO IT IS —

I ALWAYS GET THE HEAD DRAWN FIRST (MAKING SURE THAT I'VE CAPTURED THE LIKENESS)

THEN I DRAW THE BODY ACTION SEPARATELY —

I THEN COPYPRINT THE HEAD IN TWO OR THREE SIZES, CUT IT OUT AND MOUNT THE ONE THAT LOOKS BEST ONTO THE BODY TO COMPLETE THE PICTURE...

CUT AND STICK

IF YOU ARE GOING TO USE COLOUR— EITHER INKS OR WATERCOLOUR

JUST STICK TO A GOOD OUTLINE DRAWING AND MAKE A COPYPRINT...

THEN COLOUR THE COPYPRINT (IF IT GOES WRONG YOU CAN SCRAP IT AND START AGAIN WITHOUT TEARS)

AND ALSO THERE IS NO FEAR OF INK OR FIBRE TIP SMUDGING

BLAST!

CARICATURE AND CARTOONING ARE TWO
VERY DIFFERENT PROFESSIONS — DON'T
LET ANYONE TELL YOU OTHERWISE —
A CARICATURIST HAS A SPECIAL GIFT FOR
CATCHING A LIKENESS AND PUTTING IT
DOWN ON PAPER — A FEW CARTOONISTS
ARE GOOD AT IT — BUT MANY OF US HAVE
TO STRUGGLE — HOWEVER, CARICATURISTS
TRYING TO BE CARTOONISTS RARELY
HAPPENS — THE TWO PROFESSIONS ARE
MILES APART...

IF YOU FIND YOU HAVE A NATURAL GIFT
FOR CARICATURE — STICK WITH IT —
A GOOD CARICATURIST IS ALWAYS IN
DEMAND, PARTICULARLY IF YOU CAN
DEVELOP A SOPHISTICATED STYLE OF
DRAWING TO GO WITH A CLEVER
LIKENESS... MAGAZINES LOVE THIS.

GOOD PHOTOGRAPHIC REFERENCE IS VERY IMPORTANT IF YOU WANT A GOOD LIKENESS—

SO BUILD UP A GOOD LIBRARY OF PICTURES OF FACES IN THE NEWS, FILMS & TELEVISION— COLLECT THEM LIKE STAMPS...

WHICH IS THE ALIEN?

REMBRA

DUTCH ART

IF AN ITEM ABOUT
A FAMOUS FACE
APPEARS ON THE
NEWS PAGES —

YOU CAN ILLUSTRATE
IT BY PUTTING THE
CARICATURE IN
THAT SITUATION.

THIS WAY IT'S LESS
OF A CARICATURE
AND MORE OF A
CARTOON.

THESE DAYS A LOT OF THE TABLOIDS ARE IN COLOUR—I DON'T THINK COLOUR DOES MUCH FOR CARICATURE OR CARTOONS—

A GOOD BLACK AND WHITE ILLUSTRATION HAS SO MUCH MORE IMPACT—

MAYBE I'M A TOUCH OLD FASHIONED?

BEING ABLE TO WATCH PEOPLE MOVE ABOUT ON TELEVISION CAN GIVE YOU A LOT MORE INFORMATION ABOUT A PERSON THAN JUST A STILL PHOTOGRAPH ON YOUR DRAWING BOARD.

I CONSIDER CHARLES GRIFFIN TO BE THE MASTER OF CARICATURE IN THIS COUNTRY—BELOW IS A FINE EXAMPLE OF HIS WORK—HE WAS KIND ENOUGH TO GIVE ME THE ORIGINAL WHEN I INTERVIEWED HIM FOR A BOOK ON CARICATURE.

THE Strip Cartoon

—IT JUST KEEPS ON RUNNING!

CRIPES!

THE STRIP CARTOON IS IN A CLASS OF ITS OWN WHEN WE TALK ABOUT CARTOONS...

THE CONTINUITY STRIP (CARRYING A STORY DAY BY DAY) HAS NOW ALMOST BEEN TAKEN OVER BY TELEVISION SOAP OPERAS—

HOWEVER—THE GAG A DAY STRIP STILL CONTINUES TO HAVE A HUGE FOLLOWING IN NEWSPAPERS AND MAGAZINES AROUND THE WORLD—SO IF STRIP CARTOONS ARE JUMPING OFF THE TIP OF YOUR PEN—CONCENTRATE ON THIS TYPE OF STRIP.

YOU WILL NEED TO COME UP WITH AT LEAST ONE STRONG CHARACTER THAT WILL DOMINATE THE STRIP—PLUS A GREAT IDEA FOR A THEME.

A STRONG TITLE IS ALSO NEEDED— THEN, HAVING COME UP WITH THESE ALL YOU NOW HAVE TO DO IS PRODUCE GREAT GAGS DAILY OR WEEKLY OR EVEN BOTH!

THEN—AND THIS IS THE DIFFICULT BIT. CONVINCE AN EDITOR TO RUN IT IN HIS NEWSPAPER—

BUT DON'T LET ANYONE PUT YOU OFF—IF
YOU HAVE A GREAT IDEA, PLUS THE TALENT
TO PRODUCE SUCH A STRIP—PRESS ON:

DRAW YOUR ORIGINAL ARTWORK TO
THIS SIZE: 375mm X 114mm (14¾"X4½")
THIS PANEL WILL REDUCE TO A STRIP
CARTOON IN YOUR NEWSPAPER SIZE.

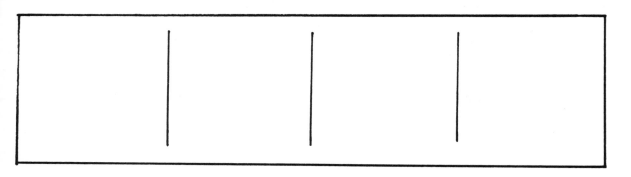

USE PEN AND BLACK INK OR FIBRE TIP OR
PILOT DRAWING PEN WITH A BRUSH FOR
SOLID BLACK—ALWAYS KEEP IN MIND
THE REDUCTION AND LEAVE GOOD SPACE
FOR LETTERING (IF THE READER CAN'T
MAKE OUT THE LETTERING—IT'S GOODBYE
TO THE GAG)

IF YOU CAN'T DO STRIP CARTOON LETTERING
JUST PENCIL IT IN AND LEAVE IT TO
SOMEONE WHO CAN (OR A COMPUTER
PRINT OUT AND PASTE) NOTHING CAN
SPOIL A STRIP LIKE BAD LETTERING—
YOU CAN EVEN GET AWAY WITH BAD,
ARTWORK IF THE GAG IS GOOD!

CAN'T READ THE LETTERING! THAT GAG WENT UP IN SMOKE

KEEP THE LETTERING TO A MINIMUM—DON'T LABOUR THE GAG—

IF YOU ARE USING SPEECH BALLOONS KEEP THEM NICE AND OPEN...

TRY AND SPACE NEAT LETTERING!

TAKE A GOOD LOOK AT THE FAMOUS STRIPS STILL RUNNING IN YOUR NEWSPAPER AFTER MANY YEARS — SEE HOW THEY KEEP THE ARTWORK AND LETTERING TO THE VERY MINIMUM TO GET THE MOST IMPACT!

THE GAG STRIP

THE DAILY OR WEEKLY GAG STRIP REQUIRES A DIFFERENT TECHNIQUE FROM THE STORY OR CONTINUITY STRIP.

IT IS BASICALLY AN EXTENSION OF A SINGLE GAG STRETCHED OUT INTO A COLUMN OF THREE OR FOUR PICTURES — EACH STRIP BEING COMPLETE EACH DAY WITH A PUNCH LINE.

THE FIRST THING YOU NEED TO DO IS CREATE A CHARACTER OR A THEME TO DEVELOP YOUR IDEAS, AN OFFICE SITUATION OR A HIS/HER DOMESTIC SITUATION, SCHOOLCHILDREN, ANIMAL CHARACTERS, ETC.

HAVING DECIDED ON YOUR THEME AND HAVING WORKED OUT YOUR MAIN CHARACTER OR CHARACTERS — THEN COMES THE DIFFICULT BIT, WORKING OUT A STRING OF SITUATIONS — GAG SITUATIONS.

I WORK OUT MY GAGS BY WRITING OUT THE DIALOGUE FIRST (ONCE YOU KNOW WHAT THEY ARE GOING TO SAY, YOU CAN THEN DRAW YOUR CHARACTERS WITH THE RIGHT EXPRESSIONS AND ATTITUDES...

ROUGH OUT YOUR PANEL OR STRIP AND ONCE YOU HAVE A GAG IDEA — WRITE IN THE DIALOGUE TO SEE IF IT WORKS, I DO SIX GAGS THIS WAY BEFORE I START TO DRAW... GET THE GAG RIGHT FIRST — THEN DRAW IT...

WHEN YOU THINK YOU'VE GOT THE DIALOGUE WORKED
OUT — THEN WORK ON THE VISUALS...

USE A LARGE LAYOUT PAD (24"x 18" approx) IT'S A NICE
SURFACE TO WORK ON WITH INK OR A FIBRE TIP —
IT'S TRANSPARENT ENOUGH TO TRACE THROUGH, SO
YOU CAN EASILY MAKE CORRECTIONS.
I SOMETIMES USE IT FOR FINISHED WORK, YOU CAN
MOUNT IT ON TO CARD FOR PRESENTATION.

ROUGH OUT THE FRAME OF YOUR STRIP TO SIZE...
(14¾"X 4½") THEN WORK OUT ABOUT A DOZEN GAGS BY
WRITING THE DIALOGUE — PICK OUT THE BEST AND
DRAW THEM UP — YOU WILL FIND THIS TECHNIQUE
USEFUL FOR JOTTING DOWN AN IDEA THAT COMES TO
YOU WHEN YOU'RE MILES AWAY FROM YOUR DRAWING
BOARD — DRAW A FRAME IN YOUR NOTEBOOK AND
WRITE DOWN THE DIALOGUE... I FIND A LONG TRAIN
JOURNEY IS PERFECT FOR MAKING GOOD USE OF
THIS SYSTEM. P.S. BUT IT'S CHEAPER TO DO IT AT HOME!

GREYHOUND—
YOU ALWAYS LOOK
HALF STARVED...

DON'T YOU
EVER GET...

HUNGRY?

NOTES...

AND SKETCHES...

A MAN KEEPS
PHONING ME UP IN
THE MIDDLE OF
THE NIGHT

HE DEMANDS THAT
I MEET HIM AT THE
PARK GATES IN
MY NIGHTDRESS

RIGHT MISS—
NEXT TIME HE
PHONES WE'LL
BE WAITING
FOR HIM

IT'S A WASTE OF
TIME, CONSTABLE
—HE NEVER
TURNS UP

YOU WILL FIND THAT AS YOU GET USED TO USING THIS WAY
OF WORKING OUT THE GAGS — ONCE YOU HAVE YOUR
CHARACTERS FIXED FIRMLY IN YOUR MIND...
THE DIALOGUE WILL FLOW VERY EASILY. — HONESTLY!

I HOPE THIS BOOK HAS WHETTED YOUR APPETITE TO ENTER THE WORLD OF THE CARTOONIST — JUST ONE WORD OF WARNING FROM ONE WHO KNOWS — IF YOU WANT TO BE RICH AND FAMOUS...

BECOME A PROFESSIONAL FOOTBALL STAR!